Warning!

Before you read this book, you should know that diving is dangerous. If you are not careful, and even sometimes if you are, you can get lost or your equipment can malfunction, and you can drown. This book explains diving but is not intended to be used as a training manual. If you plan to actually go diving, protect yourself by taking lessons, using the right equipment, always diving with a buddy, and only doing dives that you're ready for.

Also, if you do go out and get hurt or hurt anybody else, don't blame National Geographic. We didn't tell you to do it. We told you to be careful!

(Translation into legalese: Neither the publisher nor the author shall be liable for any bodily harm that may be caused or sustained as a result of conducting any of the activities described in this book.)

One of the world's largest nonprofit scientific and educational organizations, the NATIONAL GEOGRAPHIC SOCIETY was founded in 1888 "for the increase and diffusion of geographic knowledge." Fulfilling this mission, the Society educates and inspires millions every day through its magazine, books, television programs, videos, maps and atlases, research grants, the National Geographic Bee, teacher workshops, and innovative classroom materials. The Society is supported through membership dues, charitable gifts, and income from the sale of its educational products. This support is vital to National Geographic's mission to increase global understanding and promote conservation of our planet through exploration, research, and education.

For more information, please call 1-800-NGS LINE (647-5463) or write to the following address:
National Geographic Society
1145 17th Street N.W.
Washington, D.C. 20036-4688 U.S.A.
Visit the Society's Web site at www.nationalgeographic.com.

NATIONAL GEOGRAPHIC

EXTREME Sports

DIVE!

Your Guide to Snorkeling, Scuba, Night-Diving, Freediving, Exploring Shipwrecks, Caves, and more.

BY DARICE BAILER

Illustrations Jack Dickason

NATIONAL GEOGRAPHIC

WASHINGTON, D.C.

What's Inside

Extreme Sports

Part One

Going Under!

- Plunge into a New Frontier
- Shore Diving and Snorkeling
- Three Easy Pieces
- Catch the Right Train
- Scuba Doo!
- Play It Safe
- Hand Signals

Get ready to explore
another part of the world:
Start by swimming on the
surface and looking down. Get
geared up so you can dive
down into a new universe!

Plunge into a New Frontier

Take one giant stride or a backward roll off the side of a boat. Then dive into the ocean. You're weightless, as if floating in space. You can somersault like an astronaut and even swim upside down. You can hover over canyons, sinkholes, and wrecks. It may seem quiet and peaceful down here, but get ready for some pretty surprising sights.

The ocean is a kingdom stocked with more varieties of wildlife than Africa's Serengeti Plain. And if you're diving, you can get a lot closer—you can even stare some creatures in the eye. You never know what you'll see: Cruising over a reef, the hairs on your neck will spike at the sight of reef sharks. They won't come too close, but a female octopus might be bolder. She could slide a suckered tentacle along your leg, extending an underwater welcome. Meanwhile, multicolored fish swirl around you like confetti at a big parade.

COME ON DOWN!

You can enter the ocean kingdom simply by holding your breath, but you would only linger for a few minutes. To stay longer, you need a snorkel and mask. But even then you still have to keep pretty close to the surface. With an air tank, regulator, and wet suit, however, you can dive deeper and stay longer. Now you can see why the sport of underwater diving was developed—to more fully enjoy exploring the ocean depths.

CHALLENGES

The sport is full of challenges and milestones, and the best part is that you can start your training now. Teens from age 12 to 18 can learn the basics of diving with equipment *(see pp. 14–15)*. At 18, you can break away from recreational divers and join the scuba diving die-hards in technical, or extreme, diving. You can dive below the 130-foot (40-meter) recreational limit—once you have special certification, equipment, and expertise. Be the first to spot ships or submarines 240 feet (73 meters) below on the ocean floor. Sink into underwater caves so dark that a nylon rope is your lifeline back to sunlight, air, and safety. Suck in your breath and plunge on a world-record free dive.

Extreme diving isn't like diving off a board into a pool, where air is just a nanosecond away. Extreme divers make it their business to push the limits of their bodies, of their equipment, and of diving technology itself.

EXPLORE THE UNKNOWN

In the past 50 years, we have learned more about life under the sea than ever before. Yet the greatest period of underwater exploration lies ahead. Through diving, you'll be a pioneer on the Earth's last frontier. You might discover a sea urchin biologists never knew existed. Or perhaps you'll come upon some important ocean plant from which life-saving medicines can be made.

So pinch your nose and take a freedive. Or zip up your wet suit and strap on your tank. Get ready to go down!

This tropical tiger fish—also called a zebra fish—is pretty, but stay away! Its spines are poisonous!

Shore Diving and Snorkeling

You don't have to shimmy into a wet suit or snap on a buoyancy compensator device to dive. You can chase the waves out to sea, hold your breath, and dive in. You'll be doing the easiest kind of diving there is. Welcome to the world of skin diving.

When you think about it, you're already outfitted with your own natural diving equipment. Who needs air tanks or gauges when your lungs breathe in oxygen and your brain tells you when you're out of air? If you're lucky, you might be equipped with top-notch lungs like French diver Andy Le Sauce. Andy once held his breath underwater for 7 minutes and 35 seconds. The problem is, most of us don't have Andy's lung capacity. We can stay underwater only for a short while. That's where a snorkel—a breathing tube—comes in handy.

NICE 'N' EASY

Snorkeling is the next step up from skin diving. You slip on a face mask, snorkel, and fins. You can snorkel in exotic places, or in nearby lakes, bays, or oceans. It's an easy, inexpensive way to try underwater exploration. Snorkel with a buddy, just in case you get lost in an unfamiliar area or pulled by currents. Sharing the dive with someone makes snorkeling much more fun, too.

TERRIFIC REEFS

In tropical waters, snorkeling will let you explore the magic world of coral reefs. Coral comes in many shapes and sizes. Check out the hard skeletons protecting and supporting these frail organisms. Coral colors are as rich as those in a jumbo box of crayons. Brain coral looks just like a human brain! Leather coral looks like a green vegetable—one you'd never eat.

Brain Coral

CORAL REEFS NEED CARE

Coral reefs take thousands of years to form. They are brittle and fragile. Never touch, stand on, sit on, or kick the coral. Try not to stir up sand with your fins, because sand clouds can block out the sunlight corals need to make food.

Watching the show down there, you'll learn a lot. Did you know, for instance, that fish have their own "car" wash? They line up to be scrubbed by cleaner shrimp! Purple cleaner shrimp wave their white antennas, flagging the fish down. While fish wait their turn, the cleaner shrimp go to work, cleaning all the parasites and algae off each fish, one at a time.

Cleaner Shrimp

Red Coral

Three Easy Pieces

Whether you want to stick to snorkeling or train later on to scuba dive, you'll need these items of basic gear.

Mask. Your eyes can't focus in water. Why? Water is denser than air and transmits light differently. You need air space between your eyes and the water, and the mask acts like an underwater window. Try on several different masks before buying one. Look for one that feels comfortable and has a nose pocket to cover the nose completely. You also want to make sure it won't leak. Here's how: Press the mask onto your face without strapping it around your head. Breathe in and shake your head. If your mask stays glued, you've got a non-leaker. If you don't have 20/20 vision, you can wear your contact lenses inside a face mask or order one with prescription lenses.

Snorkel. An air tube about an inch in diameter lets enough air through to make breathing easy. A snorkel with a comfortable mouthpiece, or "barrel," is essential. A self-draining barrel, which clears and drains the tube, is especially helpful.

HINT

Rinse off your gear with fresh water after a salt-water dive. Dry and store your mask, snorkel, and fins out of the heat and sun.

Fins. You may feel like a duck wearing them on land, but underwater you'll swim like one, too! Look for blades that are light and flexible. Stiff blades can cause leg cramps. Try on different pairs of fins to find ones that are comfortable —but not too loose. Warm-water snorkelers go for full foot-pocket fins as opposed to open-heel ones, as these can be worn without foot-warming booties.

SNORKELING TIPS:

- Always snorkel with a buddy, so that you have help in case of an emergency.

- Perform a buddy check before you dive. Check each other's equipment. Is your mask strapped on securely?

- Quit snorkeling when you're cold—an early sign that you're getting tired.

Catch the Right Train

You've prowled a coral reef with your snorkel gear, and now you're hooked on the sea. You want to take up scuba diving and dart around like a fish. The trouble is, you'll run the risk of drowning if you attempt scuba diving without the right instruction. You've got to learn to breathe underwater and read a depth and pressure gauge.

There are many training courses you can take to earn your first certification and explore the underwater world. The Professional Association of Diving Instructors (PADI) is the largest diver training organization in the world. If you check out the Web site (www.padi.com), you can find a PADI course at a dive shop or resort near you.

At age 10, you can train for Junior Open Water Certification. It's actually the same course that's given to adults. Some resorts offer the Junior Open Water class, so you can get certified there. When you pass the course, you'll earn a certification card, that is, your license to dive. All divers need a "C-card". If you're 10 or 11, you must dive with a parent, guardian, or PADI professional, and you can't dive below 40 feet (12 meters). From 12 to 14, you can dive with any certified adult to a depth of 60 feet (18 meters). After age 15, adult supervision is no longer required.

HURRY UP!

If you want to scuba dive in a hurry, but don't have time to complete an entire course, PADI has a Junior Scuba Diver program. This is basically half of the Junior Open Water Diver course and provides a limited certification. It allows you to dive with a PADI instructor or certified dive master.

DEEPLY INVOLVED

If you're 12 or older, you can progress to the Junior Advanced Open Water Diver course. This program takes you on several different underwater adventures, such as a night dive or a deep dive to 70 feet (21 meters). You can also enroll in a Junior Rescue Diver course, where you practice surface and underwater rescues.

At age 15, you can go to your local PADI dive center to earn a full Advanced Open Water Diver certification. You'll then be qualified to leave the adults at home and dive with your qualified buddies. You can also dive to 100 feet (30 meters) and tackle more advanced diving specialties, such as deep diving, Enriched Air Nitrox diving, and wreck diving *(see p. 28)*.

SCHOOL DAYS

Besides PADI, other certifying agencies are:
- The National Association of Scuba Diving Schools (NASDS): www.nasds.com
- National Association of Underwater Instructors (NAUI) Worldwide: www.naui.org
- Scuba Schools International (SSI): www.siusa.com

A fun way to get certified is to take a three-week trip on a summer training ship such as Odyssey Expeditions. There are also charter boats that offer major certifications, such as underwater photographer and also underwater videographer.

EXTRA CREDIT

Once you get your C-card, you can tackle a specialty, such as underwater photography or videography. Some aquatic awareness specialty programs offer information about the fragile underwater ecosystem and how you can protect it. Project AWARE focuses on cleaning up beaches and preserving the ocean. Sign up for the AWARE-Fish ID course to become an expert at naming fish.

Scuba Doo!

You've learned the basics, and you're ready to go down. The question is, do you have the gear?

You can rent scuba diving equipment if you're just trying things out for a day. But if you're serious about the sport, consider buying your equipment. That way you'll know you're getting just the right gear for you.

SINGLE HOSE REGULATOR

A regulator takes the high-pressure compressed air from your tank and lowers the pressure so you can breathe it in. More advanced and expensive models inflate your buoyancy life jacket and feature a second hose to help a diving buddy who has run out of air.

Take good care of this item by flushing it with fresh water after diving. Inspect it regularly. A reddish filter means there's rust in your steel air cylinder. A blackish filter means your cylinder has a defective compressor. If you dive frequently, have your regulator serviced every six months.

BUOYANCY COMPENSATOR DEVICE (BCD)

BCDs, also known as adjustable buoyancy life jackets, help you float and keep you clear of reefs and wrecks. Most have Velcro tabs or clips to attach your regulator hose, gauges, and other diving gear. Like the wet suit, this item should fit just right. One that's too big will jostle your air tanks as it inflates and deflates. One that's too small won't hold enough air to keep you afloat. A twin-bag BCD is probably the best choice—it's durable and easy to repair.

BODY SUIT

In tropical waters, a full-body diving suit can protect you from sunburn, coral cuts, and fish stings. The suit could be a body skin—a light, one-piece suit.

In colder water, you might prefer a wet suit. This heavier suit insulates your body from cold water and keeps your body heat in your body where it belongs. Look for a wet suit with a snug fit. A baggy wet suit allows water to seep between your skin and the covering, which can be a chilling experience.

AND DON'T FORGET

You also need a . . .

DEPTH GAUGE—to measure how deep you are.

PRESSURE GAUGE—to tell you how much air is left in your tank.

DIGITAL WATCH—to tell you how long you've been under. An underwater watch should have a light for dark water and a stop watch function

WEIGHT BELT—to help you stay underwater by balancing the effect of your body's natural buoyancy, as well as the buoyancy from your BCD and your tank.

KNIFE—to cut yourself free from fishing lines, nets, seaweed, and rope. A knife with a serrated edge is best.

DIVING COMPASS—to help you find your way when diving in dark or murky water. It's like a land compass, only waterproof.

MARKER BUOY—to let others on the surface know where you're diving. This floating marker with a flag tells other boats you're down below— and it's required by law.

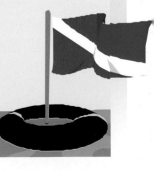

Play It Safe

You're swimming along in your undersea adventure, nose to nose with more marine life than you've ever seen. You almost feel part of this strange new world as you move around through the currents and depths, breathing easily. But as natural as you may feel, never forget that you're a visitor here. Safety is your number one concern.

Scuba diving is relatively easy to master, once you've had the proper training. It doesn't require superhuman strength, but it still involves risks. After all, you'll be spending time in environments where, without your equipment, you would not be able to survive for more than a few minutes. Be sure to keep these basic safety rules in mind at all times.

DIVING DOS AND DON'TS

DO

1. Learn all emergency procedures, including hand signals *(see p. 22)*.
2. Check out your buddy's equipment to make certain it is hooked on properly. Plan what to do if you lose track of each other underwater.
3. Drink plenty of water on the day you dive.
4. Dive within your certification limits.
5. The deepest part of your dive first. This gives your bloodstream time to rid itself of excess nitrogen as you surface gradually.
6. End a dive if you start to shiver or your arms and legs become numb from cold. Remember that the ocean is usually colder than your body temperature, so there is a risk of hypothermia—a loss of too much body heat.
7. Carry spare equipment—an extra mask, fin straps, and batteries for flashlights.

DON'T

1. Dive alone! Always dive with a buddy, parent, or dive master of a group.
2. Dive if you feel uncomfortable—never be afraid to turn back and end a dive if you become scared.
3. Dive in strong currents.
4. Swim too hard while diving. You'll use up your air supply faster.
5. Hold your breath while scuba diving. Breathe normally.
6. Exercise right before diving. Diving is hard work, and tiring yourself could be risky.

CLEARING YOUR MASK

Here's how to empty, or "clear," your mask if it fills with water while you're scuba diving:

Tilting your head back, press against the top of the mask and snort out strongly through your nose. That will force water out through the bottom of your mask. Breathe normally through your regulator.

Hand Signals

You're underwater. The only sounds are your own breathing and air bubbles rising to the surface. Suddenly, you catch sight of a brightly colored object just beyond a large rock. You want to tell your buddies about it. You're about to call out to them when you realize the mouthpiece of your regulator hose is stuck between your teeth!

On your way to getting certified, you'll learn the sign language most divers use. It's the only way to communicate when talking simply isn't an option. You can use hand signals to point out interesting or mysterious finds along the way, but you'll also need them for emergencies. Use them to tell your buddy or dive master that you're OK or low on air. Coordinate signals with new diving buddies to make sure everyone is using the same sign language. Here are the most important hand signals every scuba diver should know.

A HELPING HAND

OK

SOMETHING'S WRONG

GOING UP

GOING DOWN

LOW ON AIR

OUT OF AIR

DANGER

HELP!

TIP

You and a buddy can make up your own signals. For instance, you could form a V with your index and middle fingers and point at your eyes. This could be your code for "Look!" Then point to the item that caught your attention and invite your buddy to paddle over to check it out.

Giant clams, some weighing several tons, make permanent homes on coral reefs.

Underwater Thrills

Close-up of a large grouper

If you thought diving was only about exploring tropical coral reefs, think again. There's a whole other underwater world, full of mysteries and adventures, just waiting for you.

Lake and Quarry Diving

All set with your gear, but the Caribbean is not in your backyard? Not a problem. There's nothing to stop you from scuba diving in freshwater lakes and quarries. You never know what you might find, and you might even have the opportunity to do a good deed.

A quarry is a huge hole in the ground excavated during mining or construction. Sometimes these quarries are fed with water, and sometimes they flood. As in freshwater lakes, the water temperature in quarries is usually colder than in the ocean around Florida or in the Caribbean. The fish aren't as colorful, and the water tends to be murkier. You'll need a flashlight, and you won't be able to see as far. But you'll still find plenty of thrills and mysteries to draw you in.

SPOOKY SIGHTS

Exploring a lake underwater can offer a bit of history. Lake Michigan, for instance, is the watery grave for an old steamer ship, the *Lady Elgin,* that sank on Sept. 8, 1860. It was on its way to a rally for Stephen Douglas, who was running against Abraham Lincoln for president. That night, the ship collided with another schooner and sank.

Michigan's Isle Royale National Park, in Lake Superior, boasts six major wrecks, most of them schooners or steamships from the turn of the last century.

Not all sunken sights got there by accident. Some lakeside communities actually build attractions underwater for scuba divers to check out. Lake Travis, near Austin, Texas, features a private park that entices visiting scuba divers with an underwater cemetery (fictitious), vintage cars, and even a pecan orchard!

TREASURE HUNT

Some lakes could harbor buried treasure—you never know. Go diving to see what others have lost. You might find a diamond ring or a watch dropped by a boater back in the 1800s. And if you can't find treasure, you can always wind up doing something good for the environment. Why not scoop up some of the plastic bottle caps and soda cans littering the lake while you're at it?

FRESHWATER FLOATER

An important thing to remember when diving in lakes and quarries is that you're in freshwater, which means you'll be much less buoyant than if you were diving in saltwater. If you're accustomed to diving in saltwater, get comfortable with diving in freshwater before going on any major explorations. You'll notice that it's easier to go down and stay down, so you might want to make some adjustments to your gear. (Will you need a lighter weight belt, for example?) Also apply methods from your scuba certification course to adjust your breathing for optimum buoyancy. Try not to rely too heavily on your BCD for this purpose except when you absolutely need it.

Nighty Night

The world beneath the water's surface never sleeps. At night, the same places you visited during the daylight hours could look like a different world entirely. Whether you're using the light of a full moon or training your flashlight on the mysterious creatures around you, there's no question you've entered a mysterious and thrilling place.

It's not crazy to go scuba diving at night. In fact, it's a way to see more. In both fresh water and saltwater, marine creatures behave differently at night. Some are more active, using the darkness to hunt their unsuspecting prey. If you make a special plan to go diving at night, you won't regret it. The same rules for daytime scuba diving apply, but you'll need some special gear. Make sure that you check out your dive site during the day so you'll know your way around at night. Also, begin your dive at dusk, some time between 7 and 9 p.m. Your eyes will have time to adjust to the dimmer light.

Treefish

LIGHT UP THE LIFE

In some underwater areas, the less light there is, the more you see. In tropical habitats, fish, shrimp, and coral look like someone sprayed them with Day-glo colors. During the day, these creatures don't seem as bright, because water absorbs color. In the filtered sunlight, they appear pale and faded. But at night, you've got your flashlight shining right on crabs or shrimp, and there's much less water between the light source and the shrimp to wash out the color.

Keep in mind that you're also giving the predators a hand! Shining your flashlight on some fish puts it in the spotlight for predators such as tarpon, who may be hunting for dinner while you dive. The tarpons see the fish, and before you can count to two, the fish are gone. Just don't get between a tarpon and his dinner.

A diver displays a giant starfish.

POP GOES THE CORAL

At night, corals are hungry, too. Watch them turn upside down and feed. Their tentacles shoot up as they eat, making them look a little like neon flowers. Corals also spawn at night, releasing their eggs and sperm. Watch as the water fills with millions of tiny specks, sort of like popcorn spewing out of a popper. Wave your arm under the water, and you'll see sprinkles of light, or phosphorescence, flashing and disappearing until you disturb the water again. This is actually the light emitted by plankton, which are microscopic life-forms that drift in oceans or lakes.

NIGHT DIVING GEAR

WEAR A WET SUIT AND BOOTIES. The clothing will help you stay warm and protect you from scrapes and bruises in the dark.

TAKE ALONG TWO FLASHLIGHTS. Use one to see in front of you and a spare in case the other stops working. Buy good underwater flashlights with low power to keep from scaring marine creatures away. Make sure your flashlights are loaded with fresh batteries or are fully charged.

REMEMBER THOSE HAND SIGNALS? At night, shine your flashlight on your fingers as they form the signals. You can also turn on your flashlight and draw a circle to indicate that everything's OK. Wave your flashlight rapidly from side to side to tell your group leader that you need help.

GRAB A COMPASS! Use one with illuminated markings so that you can note your location in the dark.

Wreck Diving

Your dive master leads you to a sunken galleon—a 16th-century Spanish ship that once transported gold and jewels from South America back to Spain. Caught in a terrible storm, the ship went down in the Gulf of Mexico with all hands. Centuries later, divers uncovered the wreck and spent years removing the layers of sand over it. Now it's an attraction for divers from around the world. The treasure has long since been taken from the wreck—or has it?

Sunken treasures dot the ocean floor throughout the world. These shipwrecks often contain artifacts that are valuable clues to ways of life hundreds of years ago. Some items wind up in museum exhibitions or as heirlooms for the people who found them. But even if a shipwreck doesn't contain valuable cargo, it does tell a story. How did it sink? What became of its passengers and crew? Lucky for you, developments in scuba technology are giving present-day divers a chance to discover shipwrecks in their sandy graves and probe into these mysteries.

SALVAGER'S GOLD

In 1622, the Spanish ship the *Nuestra Senora de Atocha* set sail for Spain from the New World. It got as far as the Florida Keys, where a hurricane dashed it to pieces. The ship, containing a cargo of gold and silver coins and precious jewels, sank 54 feet (16 meters) to the bottom of the Gulf of Mexico. Almost 350 years later, in 1975, a treasure hunter named Mel Fisher dove down and salvaged $400 million in gold from the wreck. He also found a beautiful emerald cross inside a silver box. "When they popped the lid and pulled out the cross, a chill started at my foot and went up to my head," Mr. Fisher told a reporter at the Orlando *Sentinel* newspaper. Mr. Fisher had been hunting for the ship's riches for 16 years.

DEADLY CRUISE

The *Andrea Doria* was an Italian ocean liner that was called the Grande Dame of the Sea. It was 697 feet (212 meters) long, or more than two football fields in length. One foggy July day in 1956, the liner collided with another ship, the *Stockholm*, which sliced in two. Part of the boat rests 240 feet (73 meters) down in the Atlantic, about 85 miles (137 kilometers) off Nantucket, Massachusetts.

Many divers have died trying to get a look at the wreck. Diving that far down leads to nitrogen narcosis, a condition caused by nitrogen bubbles in the blood and body organs *(see pp. 52–53)*. Under pressure, the nitrogen in air becomes deadly. New gas mixtures, such as nitrox, contain less nitrogen than ordinary air. Nitrox allows divers to stay down longer and reduces the risk of nitrogen narcosis, making deep diving much safer today.

DIVERS BEWARE!

Wreck diving should only be attempted by experienced divers. There are many hazards that could prove deadly to beginning divers. Strong currents, low visibility, and dangerous passageways are just a few. In addition, many states and nations have strict laws about removing objects from sunken ships. It's best to consult a local wreck diving guide before attempting any such dive.

Divers to the Rescue

If you think it takes guts to dive underwater, imagine doing it during an ocean storm or at the scene of a plane crash or a sinking ship. The water's cold, the currents are dangerous, and there's no time to lose. You've got to dive down quickly when human lives are at stake.

The world of diving goes far beyond recreational snorkeling and scuba diving. Professional and technical divers require extensive training to dive below 130 feet (40 meters). These people help build and repair such things as bridges, oil platforms, and underwater cables. Some divers are trained to serve in air-and-sea rescue units for fire and police departments, the National Guard, and the U.S. Coast Guard. These brave people work under the most dangerous conditions imaginable, rescuing survivors of boating accidents or plane crashes. Air-and-sea units also work at sites where there are no survivors, pulling bodies from sunken ships or bringing plane wreckage to the surface for examination.

GETTING STARTED

The first step on a typical rescue mission is figuring out where to start diving. Eyewitnesses can help identify where an accident took place. The team uses buoys to mark the area for their search, and then the divers go down. Visibility is often poor, and divers have to be careful they are not wasting time by searching the same area over and over again. Other problems include underwater vegetation—divers in some freshwater areas have to make sure they don't get entangled in plants such as hydrilla, which can grow 40 feet (12 meters) or more in length. Kelp is a menace to ocean rescue divers.

FINE-TUNING TECHNIQUES

Rescue divers must be careful not to disturb the layer of silt at the lake bottom as they approach a wreckage site, which impairs visibility. They swim with their heads down and feet up, to keep their fins well clear of the silt. Rescue divers often carry other equipment—high-intensity flashlights, ropes, cutting tools—which they keep close to their bodies while swimming so it doesn't get squashed in wreckage.

WHO'S IN CHARGE?

Every search-and-rescue operation has at least one team leader—a dive master, if the operation starts from a boat, and a shore master, if it's launched from land—to make critical decisions in dangerous conditions. This person, usually the team member with the most search-and-rescue experience, coordinates lifts of survivors and wreckage from the water and monitors the positions and diving times of the others.

One member of the team is in charge of keeping a record of what is found and where. This information might go in a series of diagrams and drawings, a map of the area, or a series of photographs. Significant finds are also marked by buoys.

Extreme Diving

Ever wonder what's really down there? In the mood to venture deeper and farther than you thought possible? Meet some people who've been there, who've taken diving to new extremes.

Cave Diving

You're paddling through a tunnel bored out by hot lava that once spewed out of a volcano. The water feels glacier-cold, even through your wet suit. It's dark, so you can't see without a flashlight or headlight. You're hundreds of feet from the cave entrance and even further away from air and sunlight. If you're looking for the extreme end of this extreme sport, you've found it: cave diving.

Needless to say, cave diving isn't for everyone. In fact, if you're not at least 18—and fully trained—forget it. But no matter how old you are or how long you've been diving, cave diving requires top-flight equipment, a highly developed sense of direction, and strong survival instincts.

WHERE DARKNESS RULES

If something goes wrong on a shallow, open-water dive, you can race to the surface for air. That's not possible in an underwater cave. You have to swim out before you swim up. Not only that, but it's dark. Even in an underwater cavern—basically a cave with more light—you still need to keep your wits when exploring.

ANCIENT HISTORY

Some of the best cave diving in the U.S. is done in the limestone formations of Florida. Limestone is a type of rock formed from the fossilized remains of ancient sea creatures. The action of water currents, ground movement, and surface weather over millions of years has created a massive network of sinkholes, underground caves, and tunnels. People have known of these formations since the first Native Americans lived in Florida. It wasn't until scuba equipment was widely available in the 1950s, however, that the Florida caves became a diver's delight.

Many exciting discoveries have since been made. In 1954, a group of college-student divers explored the Wakulla Cavern in northwest Florida. Up until that time, only one diver had ever been bold enough to take a look. They came upon a leg bone measuring four feet (one meter) long. It turned out to be the bone of a mastodon, a prehistoric elephant that had been extinct for 11,000 to 12,000 years. It was the first sign of a graveyard of prehistoric beasts within the underwater cave network, a major find for scientific research.

In 1958, underwater explorer William Royal was diving in the Warm Mineral Springs in Florida. He found several bones that seemed to be part of one skeleton near an ancient human skull. Those bones were examined by scientists and determined to be over 10,000 years old—the oldest skeleton ever found in the southeastern United States. Maybe one day you will scuba dive to find your own prehistoric remains—changing what we know about the time line of history.

Stalactites in an underwater cave

Cave Raider No.1

Who was the bravest cave diver of all? That's easy— Sheck Exley.

Sheck Exley lived his life dangerously, setting records throughout his diving career. He also did a great deal to make cave diving safe for other cave divers brave enough to follow in his footsteps. Born in Florida in 1950, Exley started diving at 16. He kept on diving until he died on a dive in Mexico on April 6, 1994.

SURVIVING A SINKHOLE

On April 1, 1988, Exley went down into a sinkhole, a deep underwater hole in the ground, inside a cave in Mexico. It seemed to burrow into the Earth forever, a straight vertical shaft. One diver had gotten as far down as 656 feet (200 meters) in this tunnel, setting a world record. Exley knew if he went farther, he risked death from the nitrogen that would bubble up in his blood. To avoid that, he would need to breathe different mixtures of gas. On his way up, he calculated he would have to make 52 decompression stops to clear out the nitrogen. Even with these precautions, he knew he had only a 50-50 chance of making it back alive. And if something went wrong, no one would be able to save him.

In 17 minutes, Exley plunged 660 feet (201 meters) down in the hole to the end of his fixed line. He continued to what he thought was a depth of 690 feet (210 meters). Then he started back up. With all the decompression stops, Exley did not surface until 10 hours and 43 minutes after the dive began. He came out with his skin horribly wrinkled. Barely able to walk, Exley collapsed. But he determined that he'd dived down 780 feet (238 meters), breaking the world record. His skin and health soon returned to normal, and the next year, Exley went back. He topped his own record by diving 867 feet (264 meters) down in the same sinkhole.

DOWNSIZING THE DANGERS

Here are some basic tips from Exley's cave-diving manual, *Basic Cave Diving: A Blueprint for Survival.* But don't be fooled. Cave diving is extremely dangerous. Exley drowned in his attempt to go deeper than 1,000 feet (305 meters).

- Be triply prepared. Don't just take a flashlight and a backup, take along a third spare, too.

- Watch the air supply and stick to a rule of thirds: get down to the cave after using up a third of the air supply, use a third to swim into the cave, and a third to return to the surface.

- Wear an extension hose on your breathing regulator so that you can share air with a buddy who might desperately need air to make it back to the surface.

- Use rope: A nylon rope starting at the cave entrance will act as a safety line so that you won't get lost in the maze of dark tunnels.

THIS CAVE IS VERY DANGEROUS AND REQUIRES SPECIAL PROCEDURES AND EQUIPMENT
DIVERS DIED HERE
YOUR DEATH MAY CAUSE ALL SPRINGS TO BE CLOSED
THINK!

Warning signs like this have been placed near the entrances of underwater caves in Florida.

Ice Diving

You fall through a hole and suddenly you're surrounded with cold water—but you don't feel it. You look up at a "ceiling" where dull sunlight filters through. Your buddies are standing above you, and you can see forever!

What's extreme about diving if you're doing it in the winter? Well, it's extremely cold, for one thing. But if you're dressed for cold, you can see a lot in the icy world. It might take a little more work and coordination, but it's worth it.

GROUP THERAPY

Rather than going with just one buddy, you need a group of at least six people for ice diving. All should be certified for advanced open-water diving. You'll each have to cut a hole in the ice to get started. Cutting a hole with a 3-foot (1 meter) diameter through a foot or two of ice takes time and energy. People-power is also needed to clear snow from [the ice] around the hole, to allow more light through for the divers.

Divers take turns going down. Each is attached to a rope; the others in the group act as line tenders. One member stands by as the safety diver, ready to dive in if there's trouble. Naturally, ice divers don't stay down as long as warm-water divers. Count on being under no more than 20 or 30 minutes. Water temperatures are usually just above freezing—34°F (1° C) or so.

For penguins, ice diving is a way of life.

ICE DIVING GEAR

In addition to standard scuba gear, ice divers need:

- Dry suits. This fits more loosely than a wet suit to allow room for insulated clothing.
- Cold-water regulators. "Regular" regulators are built for warmer water and will become coated with ice when exposed to wintry air while wet.
- Special clothing. You'll need a hood and three-fingered mitts.
- Extras. Keep an extra air cylinder handy for emergencies.

FUN 'N' GAMES

Why ice dive? Ice diving might be cold, uncomfortable, and challenging, but it also gives you much better visibility underwater. At cold temperatures, vision won't be clouded by algae and microscopic life-forms that make warmer water murky.

And some things actually make ice diving more fun. Once you're under, you can do tricks such as standing upside down, treating the bottom of the ice layer as your "floor." It doesn't stop there: Place your fins against the ice layer, then signal on the rope for your line tenders to pull you towards the hole. Soon you're off! Think of it as upside-down water skiing—on ice!

Freediving: Going So Low

In freediving, you're "free" because you're not wearing heavy, awkward equipment. It's wonderful for ocean exploring! You can swim alongside manta rays without scuba gear to scare them away, and you can explore the reefs with ease. Of course, you have to hold your breath. Unless you are a fish.

In freediving competition, there are six events. In some, divers plunge into the ocean as deep as possible on a single breath of air. Other events take place in a swimming pool. In one, divers swim underwater in the pool. In another, they hold their breath while floating face down. Obviously freediving champions are people with enormous lung capacity.

Freediver Brett LeMaster tries for a world record.

HOLD IT A MINUTE!

Freedivers must be in top physical condition to dive straight down for as long as a minute and then have enough strength—and air—to swim back to the water's surface. Although competitive freediving is "free" of breathing devices, special equipment is used during freediving contests.

Competing divers use marked measurement cables to tell how far down they have gone. In most cases, weights, called ballast, are attached to the wrists to make the descent easier. In the most extreme event, a diver is strapped to a weighted sled called an immersion sled. An inflatable lift bag automatically fills with air to help the diver return to the surface faster. An easier dive? Not exactly. The immersion sled allows a diver to go much deeper, so he or she will need plenty of help getting back to the surface safely. Remember, the sled doesn't breathe for the divers, they have to dive and return in one big breath.

Each year, a few freedivers drown in their attempts to reach record depths. Play it safe, and don't practice freediving without a buddy or parent to watch.

FREEDIVING COMPETITION CATEGORIES

CONSTANT BALLAST: Weights bring down the measurement cable, and the diver carries them back to the surface.

VARIABLE BALLAST: The diver descends with weights but abandons them on the way back up.

NO-LIMITS (ABSOLUTE) BALLAST: The diver slides down in a weighted sled, then ascends with the help of an inflatable "lift bag."

Seals can remain underwater for several hours at a time.

41

They're Tops at the Bottom

Brett LeMasters and Tanya Streeter give a deep new meaning to a thrilling sport.

t takes something special to be a freediving champion—super lung capacity, great physical conditioning, and absolutely no fear. These two have what it takes—in extreme amounts.

Tanya Streeter

TANYA'S TRIUMPH

Diving came naturally to Tanya Streeter, who grew up on Grand Cayman Island. As a kid, she enjoyed diving for pretty seashells way down below, and when she got older, she began training for real. Every day she set out for a two-hour run or bike ride. Streeter also spent three hours a day in the water, practicing deep dives or swimming laps in the pool while holding her breath.

All that practice paid off. On May 11, 2001, Streeter set her sixth freediving world record. She dove down in the ocean and grabbed a 230-foot (70-meter) marker before racing back up for air, having plunged 33 feet (10 meters) deeper than any woman had before. And she stayed underwater for 2 minutes and 36 seconds.

TAKE A DEEP BRETT

On November 22, 1999, an American named Brett LeMaster took a deep breath and dove into the deep blue sea surrounding the Cayman Islands. These tiny Caribbean islands lie less than 200 miles (322 kilometers) south of Cuba. LeMaster wore a wet suit, plastic fins, and wrist weights. He competed in an event called constant ballast. In this competition, the diver must head down and back without any help. LeMaster needed to judge how far he could nosedive while saving enough strength to make it back to the surface. Two minutes and 50 seconds after the clock started, LeMaster skyrocketed to the surface, gasping for air. He dove 266 feet (81 meters) deep to set a new world record. His distance was about the length of a football field and back.

BLACKOUT

Setting the record wasn't easy. The deeper LeMaster went, the greater the pressure inside his nose and ears. He could have suffered pain and injury if he had not practiced diving to such depths.

LeMaster also risked drowning on the ride up. The reason: shallow water blackout. Deep down, water compressed against LeMaster's chest, including his heart and lungs. His heartbeat slowed and his lungs shriveled. As less oxygen reached his brain, LeMaster was in danger of losing consciousness. But as he neared the surface at the end of his dive, water pressure eased and he was safe.

A freediver explores a shallow reef.

Deep-Sea Diving

- Down, Down, Down
- Jacques Cousteau

We owe a lot to deep-sea diving's early pioneers. Without their contributions, which led to the development of today's scuba equipment, we'd be stuck on the water's surface, looking down, but seeing little.

Down, Down, Down

Famed ocean explorer Sylvia Earle, with the American flag and National Geographic banner at her side, moves about the deepest ocean in the Jim suit.

Take a quick tour through the history of deep-sea diving. Many trials (and errors) got us down to where we are today.

Through the ages, a dive was only as good as the diver's ability to hold his or her breath. Until people developed ways to breathe underwater and protect themselves from the cold, dives were short and dangerous. All that's changed now, thanks to the development of scuba equipment. The latest technology even allows professional divers to descend more than 1,000 feet. Here's how we got down there.

BEHOLD THE DEPTHS

1936: Three Frenchmen—Philippe Tailliez, Frederic Dumas, and Jacques Cousteau—experimented with watertight goggles for swimming underwater.

HOODS, BELLS, AND HOSES

The earliest deep-sea diving gear enclosed divers in protective cases and supplied air through a hose at the top. In 1690, astronomer Edmond Halley (Halley's Comet is named for him) designed an upside-down wooden barrel and waterproof hood that carried divers 50 to 60 feet (15 to 19 meters) beneath the ocean. Divers in Halley's Bell, as his contraption was called, could walk on the seabed for over an hour. The next innovation came in 1844, when French zoologist Henri Milne-Edwards designed a diving helmet with an air tube, modeled after a firefighter's smoke hood. Edwards was the model for Professor Aronnax, the narrator of Jules Verne's science fiction novel, *Twenty Thousand Leagues Under the Sea.*

BREATHING FREE

The next big leap came when inventors developed watertight helmets and suits, giving divers more freedom of movement. The final hurdle was to find a way for divers to take their air supply with them. In 1865, two Frenchmen, mining engineer Benoît Rouquayrol and navy lieutenant Auguste Denayrouze, patented a tank containing compressed air, which could go on a diver's back. Their invention laid the groundwork for modern scuba equipment, which another French naval officer named Jacques Cousteau would revolutionize in the next century (*see pp. 48–49*).

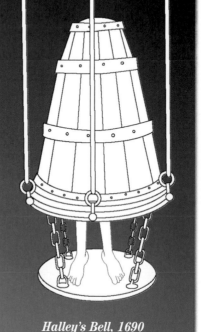

Halley's Bell, 1690

A SUIT CALLED JIM

Scientific research, wreck salvage, and search-and-rescue operations all require divers to go deep for a long time. Their bodies need special protection against the intense pressure that surrounds them on these dangerous, though necessary, missions. At 33 feet (10 meters) underwater, a diver is already facing twice as much atmospheric pressure as at the surface.

Recognizing this problem, two British engineers, Mike Borrow and Mike Humphrey, got to work on the world's first atmospheric diving suit (ADS) in the mid-1960s. They teamed up with Joseph Peress, who 30 years earlier had invented a deep-sea diving suit made of flexible materials that provided the protection needed at great depths. The so-called Jim suit, named after Jim Jarratt, the first diver to try it out, opened the way to deep dives. Scientific researchers and navy rescuers have been using Jim suits for their work ever since. The average Jim suit weighs 1,000 pounds (454 kilograms) and allows divers to go down 2,000 feet (609 meters).

Jacques Cousteau

Meet the man who made scuba diving possible, and who dedicated his life to exploring life under the sea.

A French naval officer named Jacques Cousteau made the greatest contribution to the sport of deep-sea diving, turning a life-long obsession with the seas into a career as naturalist and explorer that made him a household name. Born in France in 1910, Cousteau joined the French navy at the age of 20. His life changed when he first swam underwater with water-tight goggles.

THE AQUA-LUNG

From that point on, Cousteau was determined to find a way to dive deeper and stay underwater for longer periods. He began working with friends to develop insulated body suits and portable breathing devices. His goal: to devise a self-contained underwater breathing apparatus (now known as scuba), allowing divers to explore the ocean world.

The breakthrough came in 1943 when, with French engineer Emile Gagnan, Cousteau adapted a valve from an automobile fuel tank so that it could feed compressed air to a diver at the slightest intake of breath. Patented as the Aqua-Lung, the device revolutionized deep-sea diving and became the forerunner of today's scuba regulators.

EXPLORER OF THE SEAS

In 1950, Cousteau bought a ship that had cleared underwater mines (explosive devices) planted during World War II. He converted the run-down minesweeper into an ocean exploration vessel, "The Calypso," which he sailed to oceans around the world.

Cousteau originally set out to study marine life, as well as to develop more specialized equipment for undersea exploration. His life's work led to a wealth of discoveries about the world's oceans that Cousteau shared with the world. In a career spanning five decades, Cousteau produced a series of television documentaries, made movies, and wrote books about life in "The Undersea World of Jacques Cousteau."

As his exploration continued, however, Cousteau became aware of the great danger the world's oceans faced. Overfishing, development, and pollution took increasingly serious tolls on the planet's oceans during Cousteau's life. As a result, he was one of the first marine environmentalists, warning all that would listen that continued harm to the ocean would threaten human existence.

To further his environmental goals, Cousteau formed the Cousteau Society in 1973. His goal was to publicize the dangers that threatened Earth's oceans and support environmental programs focused on protecting the 70 percent of the planet that is water.

Cousteau pursued that goal, traveling the globe in the Calypso until he was in his late 70s. When he died in 1997, his funeral was attended by political leaders from many nations. Many who looked to the slight French explorer would agree with the inscription on a National Geographic Medal presented to him by President John Kennedy in 1961:

"To earthbound man he gave the key to a silent world."

Diving and Your Body

- I Can't Take the Pressure
- Conditioning

Part of the thrill of going underwater is being somewhere that seems impossible for humans to live. But you're swimming, you're breathing . . . you're alive. Here's how to build your body for the trip to another world.

I Can't Take the Pressure

Diving is always a thrill. But while you're caught up in the excitement of being in a different world, you can never completely shake the feeling of danger. What are the risks?

Scuba diving is safe if you stay within your recommended diving limits and dive with a parent, buddy, or group. It gets risky when you dive alone or below the 130-foot (40-meter) recreational depth limit. What are the dangers? You might've heard some diving buzz words: nitrogen bubbles, the bends, nitrogen narcosis. After a deep-sea dive, technical divers might moan, "I'm bent!" or "I got narced out!" What are they saying? How does water pressure affect our bodies?

THE BIG SQUEEZE

Ever dive off a high board into a pool? You may have felt a sharp pain in your ears when you hit the water. What happened? When you dive, water presses against your body. The deeper you dive, the greater the pressure. Your body is built with air spaces in your ears and sinuses, and these spaces squeeze as you descend. Water pressure forces your ear drums inward, causing pain in your middle ears. You can equalize your ears and ease that pain. Close your mouth, pinch your nose, and then exhale gently through your nose. After some practice, you should be able to equalize the pressure in your ears simply by swallowing.

DAZED GOIN' DOWN

Atmospheric air consists of 78 percent nitrogen, 21 percent oxygen, and 1 percent other gases. Most of the air we breathe is nitrogen, which is harmless when air pressure is normal. When we breathe in an altered pressure environment, however, nitrogen becomes a problem. The deeper we dive, the more nitrogen our tissues absorb. These tiny bubbles of nitrogen interfere with the transfer of information through our nervous system. We become less coordinated and can't think very clearly. It's a condition called nitrogen narcosis. Each diver is different, so there's no standard depth table to indicate when a diver will suffer from nitrogen narcosis. One diver might get it at 100 feet (30 meters), while a buddy might experience it a few feet deeper. But everyone gets hit with nitrogen narcosis by 165 feet (50 meters).

THE BENDS

Surfacing has its own effect on the body. When a diver ascends, the nitrogen in the body is released from the tissues. If the diver surfaces too quickly, the extra nitrogen forms bubbles in the bloodstream. Under pressure, these bubbles of nitrogen can combine to form larger, more deadly ones. They can block the flow of blood through the veins to the heart, and can lodge in the joints, causing pain or temporary paralysis. Divers call this the bends, or decompression sickness.

New mixtures of gas, such as nitrogen, helium, and oxygen, can help prevent nitrogen narcosis and decompression sickness, but these are still serious risks. Technology only keeps divers partially safe; the best prescription is to dive within your ability level—and never dive alone.

Conditioning

You're an amazing marine machine: swimming, gliding, diving, and maneuvering. You're breathing easily through your equipment, and it all feels so natural. Why? Because you're fit.

Ever swim a lap or two of freestyle and find yourself gasping for breath at the end of the pool? Then you know how tiring water sports can be. Being physically fit will give you the stamina you need to hang in there when diving conditions aren't ideal. The good news is that you can get in shape for diving and build up your cardiovascular endurance by simply playing hard at what you normally do. If you're on a sports team, you're already exercising every week. If not, consider developing a workout routine such as running, bicycling, or swimming.

EVERYBODY INTO THE POOL

You must be able to swim in order to dive, but you don't have to be a state champion. You'll want to be able to swim eight laps or tread water for ten minutes without stopping. If you haven't taken a swimming class since pre-school, taking swimming lessons and water safety classes—including lifeguard training—will help you build up your strength and breathe easier in the water.

If you are already a good swimmer, why not join a swim team at a summer club or the local Y? Swimming is an especially effective way of becoming physically fit because most of the body's muscles get a workout. Another bonus is that swimming will help you feel more comfortable in the water. It's only natural to be a little anxious about breathing underwater, but the more you swim, the less you'll have to worry about that first time you go under.

SHAPE UP

Here are other ideas for keeping in shape:
- Invite a friend over to go biking. Ride the hills around town, or hop on your mountain bike and hit the woods.
- Click on a stopwatch and time yourself and a buddy on a mile run.
- Look out for a pick-up game of basketball on your street or in your neighborhood.
- Jump rope for a couple of minutes. It's one of the best cardiovascular workouts around!

ON THE DAY YOU DIVE

- Make sure you get a good night's sleep so you'll be rested and alert.
- Don't exercise beforehand. Skip a run you might have planned. Don't tire yourself out before you dive.
- To avoid stomach cramps, don't eat a heavy meal right before diving.
- Drink several glasses of water and stay away from drinks that are carbonated or sweet, such as soda, or caffeinated.
- Don't dive if you have a cold or allergy. Any congestion will make it tough to equalize your ears.
- Avoid these medications: sleeping pills, seasickness pills, tranquilizers, antihistamines, anti-diarrhea medicine. All can cause nitrogen narcosis, even in shallow water.

DID YOU KNOW

Alcohol interferes with your ability to think and increases the risk of decompression sickness. Cigarettes prevent lungs from taking in oxygen. So don't smoke or drink—go diving instead.

Ready, Set—Dive

You've learned the ropes, you've gotten certified, and you're ready to go. You're part of a community now, a worldwide membership in one of life's great adventures. Now find out where the sights and scenes are best.

Sea Sportsmanship

You're in awe every time you dive. The ocean is full of surprises. Remember that it's important to protect the ocean so that you and your buddies can feel excitement for years to come.

As a diver, you have a responsibility to respect these natural surroundings. Although viewing marine environments as a diver is more thrilling, it's also a privilege. Never forget that you are a guest underwater.

RULES DOWN BELOW

Follow these rules for responsible diving in the world below.

- **Don't bother the fish unnecessarily.** You're there to look, not to interact. Any disturbances could affect the animals' life cycles and self-defense. Be especially careful around them; some fish have a layer of mucous on their skin that protects them from infection.
- **Don't ride the sea turtles, manta rays, or whale sharks.** They are not designed to take human cargo, and too heavy a load could harm them.
- **Look, but don't take.** Marine ecosystems are delicate, so leave shellfish and other organisms where you find them. Also, don't remove items from a wreckage site.
- **Keep the waters clean.** Report any fuel, garbage, or sewage spills you notice on your dive.
- **Wear biodegradable sunscreen.** Avoid lotions and perfumes that are harmful to underwater environments.
- **Don't feed the animals.** You don't know what these creatures like to eat; don't tempt them with something that might be harmful.
- **Use a marker buoy.** It tells people at the surface that you are diving below.
- **Don't litter.** Take out your trash from the dive boat. Throw it in a garbage can on land so that it doesn't end up in the ocean.

Caribbean Reef Shark

SOME FUN FACTS ABOUT MARINE LIFE

Whales don't get the bends. They can go down deep—anywhere from 3,000 to 8,000 feet (914 to 2438 meters) and stay down there for two hours or more. They don't get the bends because they don't breathe compressed air. Instead, they hold their breath while they're underwater.

Watch out for sharks. Fewer than ten of the more than 360 species of sharks actually pose a threat to humans, but these can be dangerous. Sharks are fascinating to watch—from a distance. Some diving facilities even offer guided shark dives.

Some fish sleep, too. They may not look as though they are sleeping, because fish have no eyelids to close. But if you notice them moving very slowly or not at all, they could be snoozing.

America's Best Diving: The Florida Keys

From the air, they could be a string of pearls. But you're not interested in seeing the Florida Keys from the air. What you want is a first-class seat below the water's surface!

The Seven-Mile Bridge connects the major islands in the Florida Keys. The older highway (right) was converted to a fishing pier and pedestrian walkway.

The Florida Keys extend into the Gulf of Mexico from the southwestern tip of the state. They are part of a huge reef that offers an abundance of marine life and attracts divers from all over the world. The barrier reef, the third largest reef in the world, is in shallow water. In fact, the Florida Keys feature the only coral reef on the U.S mainland. It hosts spectacular displays of unusual corals, including brain coral and sea fans.

FLORIDA

Key Largo

Florida
Bay

Plantation Key

Gulf of
Mexico

Long Key

Big Pine Key   Grassy Key

Key West National
Wildlife Refuge

Florida Keys National Marine Sanctuary

Atlantic
Ocean

Key West

KEY ISLANDS IN THE KEYS

Some of the islands in the Keys include Key Largo, Plantation Key, Long Key, Grassy Key, Big Pine Key, and Key West. Each island has its own particular history and attractions for visitors. All offer spectacular sights of the reef for divers in the Florida Keys National Marine Sanctuary.

For divers interested in history, the reef has been a hazard for many ships over the past several hundred years. At least ten wrecks sit on the seabed, with one dating as far back as 1733. Some got there on purpose: local communities sank a Coast Guard cutter, the *Duane,* and a Navy transport ship, the *Spiegel Grove*—to build artificial reefs and encourage more coral to grow naturally.

DIVING CAPITAL

Key Largo, the closest island to the mainland, is known as the diving capital of the world. It offers several protected underwater areas. Visit the Jon Pennekamp Coral Reef State Park, which encompasses most of the east coast of the island, for first-rate views. For other natural wonders, dive through the crystal clear waters of the Molasses Reef, or explore the underwater caves of French Reef, also on the east coast.

RULES DOWN BELOW

- **Be extra careful around coral reefs.** Coral is encased with a special mucous that helps protect it from the environment. One accidental or careless touch could damage this layer for good.

- **Watch your scuba gear.** Be careful not to whack the delicate coral reefs with your air tank.

- **Don't crash into the coral on a too-quick descent.**

- **Don't stand on the reefs at anytime.**

- **Watch your fins near the coral reefs.** Ease up on your kicking. A surge of water from your fin strokes can damage the reefs and their delicate organisms.

Queen Angelfish

Exotic Places

Scuba diving is an ideal activity for travel. Explore diving possibilities for your next vacation, or make diving the reason you fly to distant oceans. Pack your gear and take a trip!

The best diving destinations the world has to offer are prized for many reasons. They feature dramatic underwater terrain, a large variety of marine life, warm temperatures, excellent visibility, and facilities for guides and diving boats. Here are two particular international favorites.

Giant moray eel in the Red Sea.

GRAND CAYMAN ISLANDS

According to Brett LeMaster, the Caymans are the best place to dive in the Caribbean, thanks to the weather, temperature, and clear water. Natural sponges are a big draw—they come in bright colors and incredible shapes. Chances are, you've never seen anything quite like the Orange Elephant Ear Sponge or Green Rope Sponges, but you'll know immediately how they got their names. Other exciting examples of marine life include stingrays and sea turtles. Seasoned divers are also drawn to the many underwater caves surrounding the islands.

The Caymans are particularly well-geared to serve the diving enthusiasts who go there. Local facilities provide excellent diving instruction for all the training you'll need, plus guide and guideboat services.

THE RED SEA

One day, you might want to fly to the Middle East with your family and go diving in the Red Sea, many divers' choice as the No. 1 spot in the world. The water is amazingly clear, giving visibility as far as 164 feet (50 meters). The temperature is warm, and 10 percent of all the fish species in the world call this sea their home.

You can spend hours just snorkeling, and the area is ideal for an easy scuba dive. In addition to the great variety of marine life, you can explore an old shipwreck from World War II, the Italian ship *Umbria*.

Whitetip Reef Shark found in the Red Sea

SEVEN WONDERS OF THE UNDERWATER WORLD

Some are for professional divers only, but make a note. Someday you might find yourself exploring one of these places.

- **BELIZE BARRIER REEF:** Off the east coast of Belize; the second-longest reef in the world (after Australia's Great Barrier Reef); great variety of marine life; much of the reef is unexplored.
- **LAKE BAIKAL IN SIBERIA:** Great freshwater location; boasts more than 50 varieties of fish; deepest lake in the world, at 5,371 feet (1,637 meters).
- **GALAPÁGOS ISLANDS:** Chain of volcanic islands in the Pacific Ocean; home of many species that exist nowhere else in the world.
- **AUSTRALIA'S GREAT BARRIER REEF:** The longest reef in the world—as large as the state of Texas! Hands-down the best reef experience out there, at 1,250 mi long (2,012 km).
- **DEEP OCEAN VENTS OF THE MID-OCEAN RIDGE:** For marine researchers and oceanographers only. Ocean vents are openings below the Earth's crust that heat the water hundreds of degrees.
- **PALAU:** an island country in the south Pacific spread over 400 miles (644 kilometers) of ocean; several islands surround a vast lagoon, home of the world's highest concentration of tropical marine plant and animal life.

Digging Deeper

There are hundreds of books to read about diving and many excellent Web sites, too!

ADDITIONAL INFORMATION ON DIVING

BOOKS

Bane, Michael. *Diving on the Edge: A Guide for New Divers.* Lyons Press, 1998
A colorful, well-organized introductory text

Boyer, Robert. *Underwater Paradise: A Guide to the World's Best Diving Sites Through the Lenses of the Foremost Underwater Photographers.*
Harry Abrams, 1999
Great photos for those who prefer dry underwater viewing

Graver, Dennis. *Scuba Diving.* Human Kinetics, 1999
A basic reference guide for all levels

Mountain, Alan. *Diver's Handbook.* Lyons Press, 1997
Reference and tips for experienced divers

Newman, John. *Diving and Snorkeling for Dummies.* Hungry Minds, Inc., 1998
Part of the enormously successful series

WEB SITES

Discovery Diving Company
www.discoverydiving.com
Web site for wreck diving with a good selection of photos

Great Outdoor Recreation Page (GORP)
www.gorp.com/gorp/activity/scuba.htm
Several pages of Web links to scuba and snorkeling sites

Professional Association of Diving Instructors
www.padi.com
Web site of the worldwide Association offers a wealth of information

Rodale's Scuba Diving magazine
www.scubadiving.com
Web site from "The Magazine Divers Trust" with numerous links and extensive photo gallery

Snorkeling Picks and Pans
www.geocities.com/TheTropics/4385/snorkel.html
Review of snorkeling sites around the world, as well as a good list of safety tips

PHOTO CREDITS

Andy & Angie Belcher: Pages 28, 38, Front Cover; Digital Stock: Pages 2, 4, 8, 18, 19, 22, 26, 43, 44, 56; Corel: Pages 6, 9, 10, 15, 16, 24, 27, 31, 32, 34, 35, 39, 41, 50, 53, 54, 58, 61b; Corbis Royalty Free: Pages 11, 29, 48, 59; PhotoDisc: Pages 12, 14, 25, 52, 60, 62, 63; Artville: Page 13; ArtToday: Page 17, 47; Douglas Spranger/35mm Stock: Page 20; MacGillivray Freeman Films: Page 32; Wes Skiles/Karst Productions: Page 36; Dan Burton Photography: Pages 40, 42; Chuck Nicklin/Al Giddings Images: Page 46

THE AUTHOR THANKS...

The author would like to thank the following people who patiently answered countless questions about scuba diving to pass on their love for the sport and the ocean to young people everywhere:
Kathleen Bailer, scuba diving instructor
David Cabrera, scuba diving instructor and biologist at the National Institutes of Health
Jack Chalk, diving manager at Captain Don's Habitat in Bonaire
Glennon T. Gingo, manager of the U.S. Freediving Team - Apnea USA
Captain Bruce H. Mackin, diving instructor for Orbit Marine Sports in Bridgeport, CT
Leroy Wickham, educational consultant for the Professional Association of Diving Instructors (PADI).

Copyright © 2002 National Geographic Society. All rights reserved. Reproduction of the whole or any part of the contents without written permission from the publisher is strictly prohibited.
Library of Congress Cataloging-in-Publication Data
Bailer, Darice.
Dive! / by Darice Bailer.
p. cm. — (Extreme sports)
Summary: Describes sport diving using SCUBA equipment and discusses basic techniques, safety tips, and good dive sites.
ISBN 0-7922-6743-5 (pbk.)
1. Diving—Juvenile literature.[1.Scuba diving. 2. Diving]
I.Title. II. Extreme sports (Washington, D.C.)
GV854.315 .P65 2001   797.2'3—dc21   2001055840

Series designed by Joy Masoff. Design and Editorial: Jack&Bill/Bill SMITH STUDIO Inc.